Push and pull

Author: Schaefer, Lola M.
Reading Level: 1.1 LG
Point Value: 0.5
ACCELERATED READER QUIZ# 34551

hx;250

Push
and Pull

by Lola M. Schaefer

Consulting Editor: Gail Saunders-Smith, Ph.D.

Consultant: P. W. Hammer, Ph.D., Acting Manager
of Education, American Institute of Physics

Pebble Books

an imprint of Capstone Press
Mankato, Minnesota

Pebble Books are published by Capstone Press
818 North Willow Street, Mankato, Minnesota 56001
http://www.capstone-press.com

Library of Congress Cataloging-in-Publication Data
Schaefer, Lola M., 1950–
    Push and pull/by Lola M. Schaefer.
    p. cm.—(The way things move)
    Includes bibliographical references and index.
    Summary: Simple text and photographs illustrate push and pull movement.
    ISBN 0-7368-0396-3
    1. Mechanics—Juvenile literature. 2. Force and energy—Juvenile literature.
[1. Mechanics. 2. Force and energy.] I. Title. II. Series.
QC127.4.S33   2000
531'.3—dc21   99-19416
                                                                        CIP

Note to Parents and Teachers

The series The Way Things Move supports national science
standards for units on understanding motion and the principles that
explain it. The series also shows that things move in many different
ways. This book describes and illustrates push and pull movements.
The photographs support early readers in understanding the text.
The repetition of words and phrases helps early readers learn new
words. This book also introduces early readers to subject-specific
vocabulary words, which are defined in the Words to Know section.
Early readers may need assistance to read some words and to use
the Table of Contents, Words to Know, Read More, Internet Sites,
and Index/Word List sections of the book.

Table of Contents

A push moves something away from you.

Hammers push nails.

Bulldozers push dirt.

Shoppers push carts.

A pull moves something toward you.

Fishers pull nets.

Dogs pull sleds.

Children pull wagons.

Carpenters push
and pull saws.

Words to Know

bulldozer—a powerful tractor with a wide blade at the front; bulldozers can push dirt, stone, snow, or sand.

carpenter—a person who builds or repairs something with wood

fisher—a person who catches fish for a job or sport; some fishers throw nets into the water and pull them up; sometimes the nets are full of fish.

hammer—a hand tool with a metal head on the end of a handle; people use hammers to push nails into wood or other materials.

nail—a narrow, pointed piece of metal; nails are made to be pounded into wood or other materials.

wagon—a toy cart with four wheels and a long handle

Read More

Bundey, Nikki. *In the Snow.* First Sports Science. Minneapolis: Carolrhoda Books, 1998.

Challoner, Jack. *Push and Pull.* Start-up Science. Austin, Texas: Raintree Steck-Vaughn, 1997.

Gibson, Gary. *Pushing and Pulling.* Science for Fun. Brookfield, Conn.: Copper Beech Books, 1996.

Gordon, Maria. *Push and Pull.* Simple Science. New York: Thomson Learning, 1995.

Internet Sites

Amusement Park Physics
http://www.learner.org/exhibits/parkphysics

Friends of a Bulldozer
http://www.komatsu.co.jp/kikki/zukan/
bull/e_index.htm

Levers
http://www.cccnj.net/~durand1/science/motion/lever

Index/Word List

Word Count: 36
Early-Intervention Level: 8

Editorial Credits
Martha E. H. Rustad, editor; Timothy Halldin, cover designer; Heidi Schoof,
  photo researcher

Photo Credits
David F. Clobes, 20
Index Stock Imagery, 1; Index Stock Imagery/Allen Russell (1992), 18
Jim Nilsen/TOM STACK & ASSSOCIATES, 14
Kent and Donna Dannen, 16
Kimberly Danger, 10
Photo Network/David Vinyard, cover
Photri-Microstock, 12
Unicorn Stock Photos/Eric R. Berndt, 8
Uniphoto, 4, 6